50 Backyard BBQ Recipes for Summer Gatherings

By: Kelly Johnson

Table of Contents

- Classic Grilled Cheeseburgers
- BBQ Ribs
- Grilled Chicken Drumsticks
- Hot Dogs with Toppings Bar
- Grilled Shrimp Skewers
- Veggie Kebabs
- Grilled Corn on the Cob
- Pulled Pork Sandwiches
- BBQ Chicken Thighs
- Grilled Portobello Mushrooms
- Bacon-Wrapped Jalapeño Poppers
- Grilled Sausages
- BBQ Meatballs
- Grilled Salmon Fillets
- Grilled Pizza
- Grilled Potato Salad
- Smoked Brisket
- Grilled Vegetable Platter
- Stuffed Bell Peppers
- Grilled Pineapple
- Grilled Flatbreads
- Spicy BBQ Chicken Wings
- Grilled Beef Skewers
- Grilled Fish Tacos
- Grilled Asparagus with Lemon
- Sweet and Spicy Ribs
- Grilled Watermelon Salad
- BBQ Pulled Chicken
- Grilled Avocado
- Grilled Sweet Potatoes
- Spicy Grilled Shrimp Tacos
- Grilled Cauliflower Steaks
- Grilled Buffalo Cauliflower
- Grilled Zucchini and Squash
- BBQ Pulled Jackfruit

- Grilled Prawns with Garlic Butter
- Grilled Lamb Chops
- Charred Brussels Sprouts
- Grilled Shrimp and Corn Salad
- Grilled Chicken Caesar Salad
- Grilled Fajitas
- BBQ Bacon-Wrapped Chicken
- Grilled Eggplant Parmesan
- Grilled Chicken Skewers with Peanut Sauce
- Grilled Sausage and Peppers
- BBQ Baked Beans
- Grilled Cajun Fish Fillets
- Grilled Peach Salad
- Grilled Lemon Herb Chicken
- BBQ Grilled Portobello Burgers

Classic Grilled Cheeseburgers

Ingredients:

- 1 lb ground beef (80/20)
- Salt and pepper, to taste
- 4 hamburger buns
- 4 slices cheddar cheese
- Lettuce, tomato, pickles, onions, and condiments of choice

Instructions:

1. **Preheat the grill**: Preheat your grill to medium-high heat.
2. **Form the patties**: Divide the ground beef into four equal portions and shape them into burger patties. Season both sides with salt and pepper.
3. **Grill the burgers**: Place the patties on the grill and cook for 3-4 minutes per side, until the internal temperature reaches 160°F (71°C). Add a slice of cheese on top during the last minute of grilling.
4. **Assemble the burgers**: Toast the buns on the grill for 1-2 minutes. Place the cooked patties on the buns and top with your favorite toppings.
5. **Serve**: Enjoy your classic cheeseburgers!

BBQ Ribs

Ingredients:

- 2 racks of baby back ribs
- 1/4 cup olive oil
- 1/4 cup BBQ sauce (your choice)
- Salt and pepper, to taste
- 1 tsp smoked paprika
- 1 tsp garlic powder
- 1 tsp onion powder

Instructions:

1. **Preheat the grill**: Preheat your grill to medium heat.
2. **Prepare the ribs**: Remove the membrane from the back of the ribs and rub with olive oil. Mix together smoked paprika, garlic powder, onion powder, salt, and pepper, and coat the ribs with the seasoning mix.
3. **Grill the ribs**: Place the ribs on the grill and cook for 2-3 hours, turning occasionally. Brush with BBQ sauce during the last 15 minutes of grilling.
4. **Serve**: Slice and serve with extra BBQ sauce.

Grilled Chicken Drumsticks

Ingredients:

- 8 chicken drumsticks
- 1/4 cup olive oil
- 2 tbsp lemon juice
- 1 tsp dried oregano
- Salt and pepper, to taste

Instructions:

1. **Preheat the grill**: Preheat your grill to medium-high heat.
2. **Marinate the chicken**: In a bowl, mix olive oil, lemon juice, oregano, salt, and pepper. Coat the drumsticks with the marinade and let them sit for at least 30 minutes.
3. **Grill the drumsticks**: Grill the drumsticks for 25-30 minutes, turning every 5 minutes, until the internal temperature reaches 165°F (74°C).
4. **Serve**: Enjoy your juicy grilled drumsticks!

Hot Dogs with Toppings Bar

Ingredients:

- 8 hot dog buns
- 8 hot dogs
- Toppings: ketchup, mustard, relish, onions, sauerkraut, shredded cheese, chili, pickles, jalapeños

Instructions:

1. **Preheat the grill**: Preheat your grill to medium-high heat.
2. **Grill the hot dogs**: Place the hot dogs on the grill and cook for 5-7 minutes, turning occasionally, until browned and heated through.
3. **Assemble the hot dogs**: Place the grilled hot dogs in buns and set up a toppings bar with your favorite condiments.
4. **Serve**: Let everyone customize their hot dogs with toppings.

Grilled Shrimp Skewers

Ingredients:

- 1 lb large shrimp, peeled and deveined
- 2 tbsp olive oil
- 2 cloves garlic, minced
- 1 tbsp lemon juice
- Salt and pepper, to taste
- 1 tsp paprika
- 1 tbsp chopped parsley (for garnish)

Instructions:

1. **Preheat the grill**: Preheat your grill to medium-high heat.
2. **Marinate the shrimp**: In a bowl, mix olive oil, garlic, lemon juice, paprika, salt, and pepper. Toss the shrimp in the marinade and let them sit for 15-20 minutes.
3. **Grill the shrimp**: Thread the shrimp onto skewers and grill for 2-3 minutes per side, until they turn pink and opaque.
4. **Serve**: Garnish with chopped parsley and serve.

Veggie Kebabs

Ingredients:

- 1 red bell pepper, cut into chunks
- 1 zucchini, sliced into rounds
- 1 red onion, cut into chunks
- 1 cup cherry tomatoes
- 1 tbsp olive oil
- 1 tsp dried oregano
- Salt and pepper, to taste

Instructions:

1. **Preheat the grill**: Preheat your grill to medium heat.
2. **Prepare the vegetables**: Thread the veggies onto skewers, alternating the different vegetables.
3. **Grill the kebabs**: Brush the vegetables with olive oil and season with oregano, salt, and pepper. Grill for 10-12 minutes, turning occasionally, until tender and charred.
4. **Serve**: Remove from skewers and enjoy!

Grilled Corn on the Cob

Ingredients:

- 4 ears of corn, husked
- 2 tbsp butter
- Salt and pepper, to taste
- Optional: paprika or chili powder for extra flavor

Instructions:

1. **Preheat the grill**: Preheat your grill to medium-high heat.
2. **Grill the corn**: Place the corn on the grill and cook for 10-15 minutes, turning occasionally, until the kernels are charred.
3. **Finish the corn**: Brush the corn with butter and sprinkle with salt, pepper, and optional paprika or chili powder.
4. **Serve**: Enjoy your flavorful grilled corn!

Pulled Pork Sandwiches

Ingredients:

- 2 lbs pork shoulder
- 1/2 cup BBQ sauce
- 1 tbsp olive oil
- 1 tsp smoked paprika
- Salt and pepper, to taste
- 4 sandwich buns
- Coleslaw (optional)

Instructions:

1. **Preheat the grill**: Preheat your grill to indirect heat or set up for slow cooking.
2. **Prepare the pork**: Rub the pork shoulder with olive oil, smoked paprika, salt, and pepper. Wrap it tightly in foil.
3. **Grill the pork**: Place the wrapped pork on the grill and cook for 3-4 hours, turning occasionally, until the pork is tender and easily shreds.
4. **Shred and assemble**: Remove the pork from the grill, shred it with forks, and mix with BBQ sauce. Serve on sandwich buns with optional coleslaw.
5. **Serve**: Enjoy your pulled pork sandwiches!

BBQ Chicken Thighs

Ingredients:

- 8 chicken thighs, bone-in, skin-on
- 1/4 cup BBQ sauce (your favorite)
- 1 tbsp olive oil
- Salt and pepper, to taste
- 1 tsp smoked paprika
- 1 tsp garlic powder

Instructions:

1. **Preheat the grill**: Preheat your grill to medium heat.
2. **Prepare the chicken**: Rub the chicken thighs with olive oil, smoked paprika, garlic powder, salt, and pepper.
3. **Grill the chicken**: Place the chicken thighs on the grill, skin-side down, and cook for 25-30 minutes, flipping halfway through. Brush with BBQ sauce during the last 10 minutes of grilling.
4. **Serve**: Remove from the grill and serve with extra BBQ sauce on the side.

Grilled Portobello Mushrooms

Ingredients:

- 4 large Portobello mushroom caps, cleaned and stems removed
- 3 tbsp olive oil
- 1 tbsp balsamic vinegar
- 2 cloves garlic, minced
- Salt and pepper, to taste
- Fresh basil or parsley, for garnish

Instructions:

1. **Preheat the grill**: Preheat your grill to medium heat.
2. **Prepare the mushrooms**: In a bowl, mix olive oil, balsamic vinegar, minced garlic, salt, and pepper. Brush the mushroom caps with the mixture.
3. **Grill the mushrooms**: Place the mushrooms on the grill, gill-side down, and cook for 4-5 minutes per side, until tender.
4. **Serve**: Garnish with fresh basil or parsley and serve as a side dish or main course.

Bacon-Wrapped Jalapeño Poppers

Ingredients:

- 12 fresh jalapeño peppers, halved and seeds removed
- 8 oz cream cheese, softened
- 1/2 cup shredded cheddar cheese
- 12 slices bacon
- Salt and pepper, to taste

Instructions:

1. **Preheat the grill**: Preheat your grill to medium heat.
2. **Prepare the poppers**: In a bowl, mix cream cheese, shredded cheddar, salt, and pepper. Stuff each jalapeño half with the cheese mixture.
3. **Wrap with bacon**: Wrap each stuffed jalapeño with a slice of bacon and secure with toothpicks.
4. **Grill the poppers**: Place the bacon-wrapped jalapeños on the grill and cook for 10-12 minutes, turning occasionally, until the bacon is crispy.
5. **Serve**: Let cool slightly before serving.

Grilled Sausages

Ingredients:

- 6 sausages (Italian, bratwurst, or your favorite type)
- 1 tbsp olive oil
- Salt and pepper, to taste
- Optional: sliced onions and bell peppers for grilling

Instructions:

1. **Preheat the grill**: Preheat your grill to medium-high heat.
2. **Prepare the sausages**: Lightly coat the sausages with olive oil and season with salt and pepper.
3. **Grill the sausages**: Place the sausages on the grill and cook for 8-10 minutes, turning frequently, until browned and cooked through.
4. **Serve**: Serve on buns with optional grilled onions and bell peppers.

BBQ Meatballs

Ingredients:

- 1 lb ground beef
- 1/4 cup breadcrumbs
- 1/4 cup grated Parmesan cheese
- 1 egg
- 2 cloves garlic, minced
- 1/2 cup BBQ sauce
- Salt and pepper, to taste

Instructions:

1. **Preheat the grill**: Preheat your grill to medium heat.
2. **Prepare the meatballs**: In a bowl, combine ground beef, breadcrumbs, Parmesan, egg, garlic, salt, and pepper. Form into meatballs (about 1-inch in diameter).
3. **Grill the meatballs**: Place the meatballs on a grill-safe tray or directly on the grill grates. Cook for 10-12 minutes, turning occasionally, until browned and cooked through.
4. **Coat with BBQ sauce**: Brush with BBQ sauce during the last few minutes of grilling.
5. **Serve**: Serve the BBQ meatballs with additional sauce on the side.

Grilled Salmon Fillets

Ingredients:

- 4 salmon fillets, skin-on
- 2 tbsp olive oil
- 1 tbsp lemon juice
- 1 tsp dried dill or fresh parsley
- Salt and pepper, to taste

Instructions:

1. **Preheat the grill**: Preheat your grill to medium-high heat.
2. **Prepare the salmon**: Drizzle the salmon fillets with olive oil and lemon juice. Season with dill (or parsley), salt, and pepper.
3. **Grill the salmon**: Place the salmon fillets on the grill, skin-side down. Grill for 4-5 minutes per side, or until the internal temperature reaches 145°F (63°C).
4. **Serve**: Serve the grilled salmon with additional lemon wedges.

Grilled Pizza

Ingredients:

- 1 pizza dough (store-bought or homemade)
- Olive oil
- Pizza sauce
- 1 cup shredded mozzarella cheese
- Toppings of choice (pepperoni, veggies, olives, etc.)

Instructions:

1. **Preheat the grill**: Preheat your grill to medium-high heat.
2. **Prepare the pizza dough**: Roll out the pizza dough on a lightly floured surface. Brush one side with olive oil.
3. **Grill the crust**: Place the dough on the grill, oil-side down. Grill for 2-3 minutes until the bottom is golden and crisp. Flip the dough over.
4. **Add toppings**: Spread pizza sauce on the grilled side, then top with mozzarella and other desired toppings.
5. **Grill the pizza**: Close the grill lid and cook for 5-7 minutes, until the cheese is melted and bubbly, and the crust is crisp.
6. **Serve**: Slice and enjoy your grilled pizza!

Grilled Potato Salad

Ingredients:

- 2 lbs baby potatoes, halved
- 2 tbsp olive oil
- Salt and pepper, to taste
- 1/2 cup mayonnaise
- 1/4 cup Dijon mustard
- 1 tbsp apple cider vinegar
- 1 tbsp fresh parsley, chopped
- 1/4 red onion, thinly sliced

Instructions:

1. **Preheat the grill**: Preheat your grill to medium-high heat.
2. **Prepare the potatoes**: Toss the baby potatoes with olive oil, salt, and pepper. Place the potatoes in a grill basket or on a foil-lined tray.
3. **Grill the potatoes**: Grill the potatoes for 15-20 minutes, turning occasionally, until they are tender and have grill marks.
4. **Prepare the dressing**: In a bowl, combine mayonnaise, Dijon mustard, apple cider vinegar, and fresh parsley.
5. **Assemble the salad**: Once the potatoes are grilled, toss them with the dressing and sliced red onion. Serve warm or at room temperature.

Smoked Brisket

Ingredients:

- 5-6 lbs beef brisket
- 1/4 cup olive oil
- 2 tbsp brown sugar
- 1 tbsp paprika
- 1 tbsp garlic powder
- 1 tbsp onion powder
- 1 tsp cumin
- Salt and pepper, to taste
- 1/2 cup beef broth

Instructions:

1. **Prepare the brisket**: Rub the brisket with olive oil, brown sugar, paprika, garlic powder, onion powder, cumin, salt, and pepper.
2. **Preheat the smoker**: Preheat your smoker to 225°F (107°C). Add wood chips of your choice for smoking.
3. **Smoke the brisket**: Place the brisket in the smoker and cook for 6-8 hours, or until the internal temperature reaches 195°F (90°C) for a tender result. Baste with beef broth occasionally.
4. **Rest and serve**: Let the brisket rest for 30 minutes before slicing against the grain and serving.

Grilled Vegetable Platter

Ingredients:

- 1 zucchini, sliced
- 1 red bell pepper, cut into strips
- 1 yellow bell pepper, cut into strips
- 1 eggplant, sliced
- 1 red onion, cut into wedges
- 2 tbsp olive oil
- Salt and pepper, to taste
- Fresh herbs (thyme, rosemary), for garnish

Instructions:

1. **Preheat the grill**: Preheat your grill to medium-high heat.
2. **Prepare the vegetables**: Toss the vegetables with olive oil, salt, and pepper.
3. **Grill the vegetables**: Place the vegetables on the grill and cook for 4-5 minutes per side, until tender and slightly charred.
4. **Serve**: Arrange the grilled vegetables on a platter and garnish with fresh herbs before serving.

Stuffed Bell Peppers

Ingredients:

- 4 bell peppers, tops cut off and seeds removed
- 1 lb ground beef or turkey
- 1/2 cup cooked rice
- 1 can diced tomatoes (14 oz)
- 1/2 cup shredded cheddar cheese
- 1 tsp garlic powder
- Salt and pepper, to taste
- 1 tbsp olive oil

Instructions:

1. **Preheat the grill**: Preheat your grill to medium heat.
2. **Prepare the filling**: In a pan, cook the ground meat until browned. Stir in the cooked rice, diced tomatoes, garlic powder, salt, and pepper. Cook for another 5 minutes.
3. **Stuff the peppers**: Fill each bell pepper with the meat mixture, pressing down gently to pack the filling.
4. **Grill the peppers**: Brush the stuffed peppers with olive oil and place them on the grill. Cook for 25-30 minutes, until the peppers are tender and the filling is heated through.
5. **Top with cheese**: In the last 5 minutes of grilling, sprinkle shredded cheese on top and let it melt.

Grilled Pineapple

Ingredients:

- 1 ripe pineapple, peeled and sliced into rings
- 2 tbsp honey
- 1 tsp cinnamon
- 1/2 tsp vanilla extract

Instructions:

1. **Preheat the grill**: Preheat your grill to medium heat.
2. **Prepare the pineapple**: Brush the pineapple slices with honey, cinnamon, and vanilla extract.
3. **Grill the pineapple**: Place the pineapple slices on the grill and cook for 3-4 minutes per side, until grill marks appear and the fruit softens.
4. **Serve**: Serve the grilled pineapple as a side dish or dessert, optionally with a scoop of vanilla ice cream.

Grilled Flatbreads

Ingredients:

- 2 cups all-purpose flour
- 1/2 tsp salt
- 1 tbsp olive oil
- 1/2 cup warm water
- 1 tsp active dry yeast
- 1/2 tsp sugar

Instructions:

1. **Prepare the dough**: In a bowl, combine warm water, sugar, and yeast. Let sit for 5 minutes until foamy. Add flour, salt, and olive oil, and knead the dough until smooth. Let the dough rise for 1 hour.
2. **Preheat the grill**: Preheat your grill to medium-high heat.
3. **Shape the dough**: Divide the dough into small portions and roll them out into flatbreads.
4. **Grill the flatbreads**: Place the flatbreads on the grill and cook for 2-3 minutes per side, until golden and puffed.
5. **Serve**: Serve the grilled flatbreads warm, with toppings like hummus or tzatziki.

Spicy BBQ Chicken Wings

Ingredients:

- 10 chicken wings
- 1/4 cup BBQ sauce
- 2 tbsp hot sauce
- 1 tbsp honey
- 1 tsp cayenne pepper
- Salt and pepper, to taste

Instructions:

1. **Preheat the grill**: Preheat your grill to medium heat.
2. **Prepare the marinade**: In a bowl, combine BBQ sauce, hot sauce, honey, cayenne pepper, salt, and pepper.
3. **Marinate the wings**: Coat the chicken wings in the marinade and let them sit for 20 minutes.
4. **Grill the wings**: Place the wings on the grill and cook for 15-20 minutes, turning occasionally, until the wings are crispy and cooked through.
5. **Serve**: Serve the wings hot with extra sauce on the side.

Grilled Beef Skewers

Ingredients:

- 1 lb beef sirloin, cut into 1-inch cubes
- 1/4 cup olive oil
- 2 tbsp soy sauce
- 2 tbsp Worcestershire sauce
- 1 tbsp garlic powder
- 1 tsp smoked paprika
- Salt and pepper, to taste
- Skewers (wooden or metal)

Instructions:

1. **Preheat the grill**: Preheat your grill to medium-high heat.
2. **Prepare the marinade**: In a bowl, combine olive oil, soy sauce, Worcestershire sauce, garlic powder, smoked paprika, salt, and pepper.
3. **Marinate the beef**: Thread the beef cubes onto skewers and coat them with the marinade. Let marinate for at least 30 minutes.
4. **Grill the skewers**: Place the skewers on the grill and cook for 8-10 minutes, turning occasionally, until the beef reaches your desired level of doneness.
5. **Serve**: Serve the grilled beef skewers with a side of dipping sauce or grilled vegetables.

Grilled Fish Tacos

Ingredients:

- 1 lb white fish fillets (such as cod or tilapia)
- 2 tbsp olive oil
- 1 tbsp lime juice
- 1 tsp cumin
- 1 tsp chili powder
- Salt and pepper, to taste
- 8 small corn tortillas
- 1/2 cup shredded cabbage
- 1/4 cup fresh cilantro, chopped
- 1/4 cup sour cream
- 1 tbsp hot sauce (optional)

Instructions:

1. **Prepare the fish**: In a small bowl, mix olive oil, lime juice, cumin, chili powder, salt, and pepper. Brush the mixture over the fish fillets.
2. **Grill the fish**: Preheat the grill to medium heat. Grill the fish for 3-4 minutes per side, until cooked through and easily flaked with a fork.
3. **Prepare the tortillas**: While the fish grills, warm the tortillas on the grill for 1-2 minutes on each side.
4. **Assemble the tacos**: Flake the grilled fish into bite-sized pieces. Place the fish in the tortillas and top with shredded cabbage, cilantro, sour cream, and a drizzle of hot sauce.

Grilled Asparagus with Lemon

Ingredients:

- 1 lb asparagus, trimmed
- 2 tbsp olive oil
- Salt and pepper, to taste
- 1 lemon, cut into wedges
- 1 tbsp fresh parsley, chopped (optional)

Instructions:

1. **Preheat the grill**: Preheat your grill to medium-high heat.
2. **Prepare the asparagus**: Toss the asparagus with olive oil, salt, and pepper.
3. **Grill the asparagus**: Place the asparagus on the grill and cook for 5-7 minutes, turning occasionally, until tender and lightly charred.
4. **Serve**: Squeeze fresh lemon juice over the grilled asparagus and garnish with parsley if desired.

Sweet and Spicy Ribs

Ingredients:

- 2 racks baby back ribs
- 1/4 cup brown sugar
- 2 tbsp paprika
- 1 tbsp chili powder
- 1 tsp garlic powder
- 1/2 tsp cayenne pepper
- Salt and pepper, to taste
- 1 cup BBQ sauce
- 2 tbsp honey

Instructions:

1. **Prepare the ribs**: Preheat the grill to medium heat. In a small bowl, mix brown sugar, paprika, chili powder, garlic powder, cayenne pepper, salt, and pepper. Rub the seasoning mix generously over the ribs.
2. **Grill the ribs**: Place the ribs on the grill over indirect heat and cook for 1.5-2 hours, turning occasionally and basting with BBQ sauce and honey during the last 15 minutes of grilling.
3. **Serve**: Let the ribs rest for 10 minutes before slicing and serving.

Grilled Watermelon Salad

Ingredients:

- 4 cups watermelon, cut into cubes
- 1 tbsp olive oil
- 1/4 cup feta cheese, crumbled
- 1/4 cup fresh mint leaves, chopped
- 1 tbsp honey
- 1 tbsp balsamic glaze

Instructions:

1. **Grill the watermelon**: Preheat the grill to medium-high heat. Drizzle olive oil over the watermelon cubes and grill for 2-3 minutes per side, just until grill marks appear.
2. **Assemble the salad**: Arrange the grilled watermelon on a platter. Drizzle with honey and balsamic glaze, then sprinkle with crumbled feta cheese and fresh mint.

BBQ Pulled Chicken

Ingredients:

- 4 boneless, skinless chicken breasts
- 1 cup BBQ sauce
- 1/2 cup chicken broth
- 1/2 tsp garlic powder
- 1/2 tsp onion powder
- Salt and pepper, to taste

Instructions:

1. **Prepare the chicken**: Season the chicken breasts with garlic powder, onion powder, salt, and pepper.
2. **Grill the chicken**: Preheat the grill to medium heat. Grill the chicken for 5-6 minutes per side, until fully cooked (internal temperature of 165°F).
3. **Shred the chicken**: Let the chicken rest for 5 minutes, then shred it with two forks. Toss the shredded chicken in BBQ sauce and chicken broth.
4. **Serve**: Serve the pulled chicken on buns or with a side of grilled vegetables.

Grilled Avocado

Ingredients:

- 2 ripe avocados, halved and pitted
- 2 tbsp olive oil
- Salt and pepper, to taste
- 1 lime, cut into wedges

Instructions:

1. **Preheat the grill**: Preheat your grill to medium heat.
2. **Prepare the avocados**: Brush the avocado halves with olive oil and season with salt and pepper.
3. **Grill the avocados**: Place the avocados cut-side down on the grill and cook for 2-3 minutes, until grill marks appear.
4. **Serve**: Squeeze fresh lime juice over the grilled avocados and serve as a side dish or appetizer.

Grilled Sweet Potatoes

Ingredients:

- 2 large sweet potatoes, peeled and cut into 1/2-inch slices
- 2 tbsp olive oil
- Salt and pepper, to taste
- 1 tsp smoked paprika (optional)

Instructions:

1. **Preheat the grill**: Preheat your grill to medium heat.
2. **Prepare the sweet potatoes**: Toss the sweet potato slices with olive oil, salt, pepper, and smoked paprika (if using).
3. **Grill the sweet potatoes**: Place the sweet potatoes on the grill and cook for 4-5 minutes per side, until tender and lightly charred.
4. **Serve**: Serve the grilled sweet potatoes as a side dish with a sprinkle of salt.

Spicy Grilled Shrimp Tacos

Ingredients:

- 1 lb shrimp, peeled and deveined
- 1 tbsp olive oil
- 1 tbsp chili powder
- 1 tsp cumin
- 1/2 tsp cayenne pepper
- Salt and pepper, to taste
- 8 small corn tortillas
- 1/2 cup shredded cabbage
- 1/4 cup cilantro, chopped
- 1/4 cup sour cream
- 1 tbsp hot sauce (optional)

Instructions:

1. **Prepare the shrimp**: Toss the shrimp in olive oil, chili powder, cumin, cayenne pepper, salt, and pepper.
2. **Grill the shrimp**: Preheat the grill to medium-high heat. Grill the shrimp for 2-3 minutes per side, until pink and cooked through.
3. **Prepare the tortillas**: Warm the tortillas on the grill for 1-2 minutes on each side.
4. **Assemble the tacos**: Place the grilled shrimp in the tortillas and top with shredded cabbage, cilantro, sour cream, and a drizzle of hot sauce if desired.

Grilled Cauliflower Steaks

Ingredients:

- 1 large cauliflower head, cut into 1-inch thick steaks
- 3 tbsp olive oil
- Salt and pepper, to taste
- 1 tsp smoked paprika
- 1/2 tsp garlic powder
- Fresh lemon wedges, for serving

Instructions:

1. **Prepare the cauliflower**: Remove the leaves from the cauliflower and slice it into 1-inch thick steaks. Brush both sides with olive oil, and season with salt, pepper, smoked paprika, and garlic powder.
2. **Grill the cauliflower**: Preheat your grill to medium-high heat. Place the cauliflower steaks on the grill and cook for 4-5 minutes on each side, until tender and charred.
3. **Serve**: Serve the grilled cauliflower steaks with fresh lemon wedges on the side.

Grilled Buffalo Cauliflower

Ingredients:

- 1 medium cauliflower, cut into florets
- 2 tbsp olive oil
- 1/2 cup buffalo sauce
- 1/4 tsp garlic powder
- Salt, to taste
- Fresh parsley, chopped (optional)

Instructions:

1. **Prepare the cauliflower**: Preheat your grill to medium heat. Toss the cauliflower florets with olive oil, garlic powder, and salt.
2. **Grill the cauliflower**: Grill the cauliflower for 5-7 minutes per side, turning occasionally, until golden and slightly charred.
3. **Coat with buffalo sauce**: In a bowl, toss the grilled cauliflower with buffalo sauce.
4. **Serve**: Garnish with fresh parsley, if desired, and serve as an appetizer or side dish.

Grilled Zucchini and Squash

Ingredients:

- 2 zucchinis, sliced lengthwise
- 2 yellow squashes, sliced lengthwise
- 2 tbsp olive oil
- Salt and pepper, to taste
- 1/2 tsp Italian seasoning

Instructions:

1. **Prepare the vegetables**: Toss the zucchini and squash slices with olive oil, salt, pepper, and Italian seasoning.
2. **Grill the veggies**: Preheat the grill to medium-high heat. Place the zucchini and squash slices on the grill and cook for 3-4 minutes per side, until tender and lightly charred.
3. **Serve**: Serve as a side dish or in a salad.

BBQ Pulled Jackfruit

Ingredients:

- 2 cans young green jackfruit in brine, drained and shredded
- 1 tbsp olive oil
- 1/2 cup BBQ sauce
- 1/2 tsp smoked paprika
- 1/4 tsp garlic powder
- Salt and pepper, to taste

Instructions:

1. **Prepare the jackfruit**: Heat olive oil in a large pan over medium heat. Add the shredded jackfruit and sauté for 5 minutes, allowing it to soften.
2. **Season the jackfruit**: Stir in the BBQ sauce, smoked paprika, garlic powder, salt, and pepper. Cook for another 5-7 minutes, until the jackfruit is tender and absorbs the sauce.
3. **Grill the jackfruit**: Transfer the jackfruit to a grill-safe tray and grill on medium heat for 5-10 minutes, turning occasionally to achieve a slightly charred effect.
4. **Serve**: Serve the BBQ pulled jackfruit on buns or as a topping for salads.

Grilled Prawns with Garlic Butter

Ingredients:

- 1 lb large prawns, peeled and deveined
- 2 tbsp olive oil
- 1/4 cup unsalted butter, melted
- 3 garlic cloves, minced
- 1 tbsp lemon juice
- 1/4 tsp paprika
- Salt and pepper, to taste
- Fresh parsley, chopped

Instructions:

1. **Prepare the prawns**: In a bowl, mix olive oil, melted butter, minced garlic, lemon juice, paprika, salt, and pepper. Toss the prawns in the marinade and refrigerate for 15 minutes.
2. **Grill the prawns**: Preheat the grill to medium-high heat. Grill the prawns for 2-3 minutes per side, until they turn pink and opaque.
3. **Serve**: Garnish with chopped fresh parsley and serve immediately.

Grilled Lamb Chops

Ingredients:

- 8 lamb chops, bone-in
- 3 tbsp olive oil
- 2 tbsp fresh rosemary, chopped
- 3 garlic cloves, minced
- 1 tbsp lemon juice
- Salt and pepper, to taste

Instructions:

1. **Marinate the lamb chops**: In a bowl, whisk together olive oil, rosemary, garlic, lemon juice, salt, and pepper. Coat the lamb chops with the marinade and let them rest for at least 30 minutes.
2. **Grill the lamb chops**: Preheat the grill to medium-high heat. Grill the lamb chops for 3-4 minutes per side for medium-rare, or longer if you prefer a more well-done steak.
3. **Serve**: Let the lamb chops rest for a few minutes before serving.

Charred Brussels Sprouts

Ingredients:

- 1 lb Brussels sprouts, trimmed and halved
- 2 tbsp olive oil
- Salt and pepper, to taste
- 1/4 tsp smoked paprika
- 1 tbsp balsamic vinegar (optional)

Instructions:

1. **Prepare the Brussels sprouts**: Toss the Brussels sprouts with olive oil, salt, pepper, and smoked paprika.
2. **Grill the Brussels sprouts**: Preheat your grill to medium-high heat. Place the Brussels sprouts on the grill cut-side down and cook for 5-7 minutes, turning occasionally, until charred and tender.
3. **Serve**: Drizzle with balsamic vinegar, if desired, and serve as a side dish.

Grilled Shrimp and Corn Salad

Ingredients:

- 1 lb shrimp, peeled and deveined
- 2 ears corn, husked and grilled
- 1 avocado, diced
- 1/2 red onion, finely chopped
- 1/4 cup fresh cilantro, chopped
- 1 lime, juiced
- 2 tbsp olive oil
- Salt and pepper, to taste

Instructions:

1. **Grill the shrimp**: Preheat the grill to medium-high heat. Grill the shrimp for 2-3 minutes per side until pink and opaque. Remove from the grill and set aside.
2. **Grill the corn**: Grill the corn on medium-high heat, turning occasionally, for 10 minutes, until charred. Cut the kernels off the cob once cooled.
3. **Assemble the salad**: In a large bowl, combine the grilled shrimp, corn, avocado, red onion, and cilantro. Drizzle with lime juice and olive oil, then season with salt and pepper.
4. **Serve**: Serve the grilled shrimp and corn salad chilled or at room temperature.

Grilled Chicken Caesar Salad

Ingredients:

- 2 boneless, skinless chicken breasts
- 1 tbsp olive oil
- Salt and pepper, to taste
- 1 tsp garlic powder
- 6 cups romaine lettuce, chopped
- 1/2 cup Caesar dressing
- 1/4 cup Parmesan cheese, grated
- Croutons, for topping

Instructions:

1. **Grill the chicken**: Preheat the grill to medium-high heat. Season the chicken breasts with olive oil, salt, pepper, and garlic powder. Grill for 6-7 minutes per side until fully cooked and juices run clear. Let the chicken rest for a few minutes before slicing.
2. **Assemble the salad**: In a large bowl, toss the chopped romaine lettuce with Caesar dressing. Add the grilled chicken slices on top.
3. **Serve**: Sprinkle with Parmesan cheese and top with croutons. Serve immediately.

Grilled Fajitas

Ingredients:

- 1 lb flank steak, sliced into thin strips
- 1 tbsp olive oil
- 1 tsp chili powder
- 1 tsp cumin
- 1/2 tsp paprika
- 1/2 tsp garlic powder
- Salt and pepper, to taste
- 1 red bell pepper, sliced
- 1 yellow bell pepper, sliced
- 1 onion, sliced
- Flour tortillas, for serving
- Lime wedges, for serving

Instructions:

1. **Marinate the steak**: In a bowl, combine olive oil, chili powder, cumin, paprika, garlic powder, salt, and pepper. Add the steak strips and toss to coat. Marinate for at least 30 minutes.
2. **Grill the fajita ingredients**: Preheat the grill to medium-high heat. Grill the steak strips for 2-3 minutes per side. At the same time, grill the bell peppers and onion for 4-5 minutes until charred and tender.
3. **Serve**: Warm the flour tortillas on the grill for a minute or two. Serve the grilled steak and vegetables in the tortillas with lime wedges.

BBQ Bacon-Wrapped Chicken

Ingredients:

- 4 boneless, skinless chicken breasts
- 8 slices bacon
- 1/4 cup BBQ sauce
- Salt and pepper, to taste
- 1 tsp smoked paprika

Instructions:

1. **Wrap the chicken**: Preheat the grill to medium-high heat. Season the chicken breasts with salt, pepper, and smoked paprika. Wrap each chicken breast with two slices of bacon.
2. **Grill the chicken**: Place the bacon-wrapped chicken on the grill. Cook for 6-7 minutes per side, brushing with BBQ sauce during the last few minutes of grilling.
3. **Serve**: Once the chicken is fully cooked, remove from the grill and serve with extra BBQ sauce on the side.

Grilled Eggplant Parmesan

Ingredients:

- 2 medium eggplants, sliced into 1/2-inch thick rounds
- 2 tbsp olive oil
- Salt and pepper, to taste
- 1 cup marinara sauce
- 1 cup shredded mozzarella cheese
- 1/4 cup grated Parmesan cheese
- Fresh basil leaves, for garnish

Instructions:

1. **Grill the eggplant**: Preheat the grill to medium heat. Brush the eggplant slices with olive oil and season with salt and pepper. Grill the slices for 3-4 minutes per side until tender and slightly charred.
2. **Assemble the dish**: Preheat the oven to 375°F (190°C). Arrange the grilled eggplant slices in a baking dish. Spoon marinara sauce over each slice, then sprinkle with mozzarella and Parmesan cheese.
3. **Bake**: Bake in the oven for 10-15 minutes until the cheese is melted and bubbly. Garnish with fresh basil leaves and serve.

Grilled Chicken Skewers with Peanut Sauce

Ingredients:

- 1 lb chicken breast, cut into 1-inch cubes
- 2 tbsp olive oil
- 1 tbsp soy sauce
- 1 tbsp honey
- 1 tsp garlic powder
- Salt and pepper, to taste
- 1/2 cup peanut butter
- 2 tbsp soy sauce
- 1 tbsp lime juice
- 1 tbsp honey
- 1/2 tsp chili flakes (optional)
- Skewers, soaked in water for 30 minutes

Instructions:

1. **Marinate the chicken**: In a bowl, mix olive oil, soy sauce, honey, garlic powder, salt, and pepper. Add the chicken cubes and toss to coat. Let it marinate for at least 30 minutes.
2. **Prepare the peanut sauce**: In a separate bowl, whisk together peanut butter, soy sauce, lime juice, honey, and chili flakes until smooth.
3. **Grill the chicken skewers**: Preheat the grill to medium-high heat. Thread the marinated chicken cubes onto the skewers. Grill the skewers for 3-4 minutes per side, until the chicken is fully cooked.
4. **Serve**: Serve the grilled chicken skewers with the peanut sauce for dipping.

Grilled Sausage and Peppers

Ingredients:

- 4 sausages (your choice: Italian, bratwurst, or chicken sausage)
- 1 red bell pepper, sliced
- 1 yellow bell pepper, sliced
- 1 onion, sliced
- 1 tbsp olive oil
- Salt and pepper, to taste
- 1 tsp garlic powder
- 1/2 tsp dried oregano

Instructions:

1. **Prepare the sausages**: Preheat the grill to medium-high heat. Grill the sausages for 6-8 minutes, turning occasionally, until fully cooked and browned on all sides.
2. **Grill the peppers and onions**: In a large bowl, toss the bell peppers and onion slices with olive oil, salt, pepper, garlic powder, and oregano. Grill them for 5-7 minutes, turning occasionally, until they are tender and slightly charred.
3. **Serve**: Serve the grilled sausages with the grilled peppers and onions on a bun or alongside as a side dish.

BBQ Baked Beans

Ingredients:

- 2 cans (15 oz each) baked beans
- 1/2 cup BBQ sauce
- 1/4 cup brown sugar
- 1/4 cup chopped onion
- 1/4 cup diced bacon or ham (optional)
- 1 tbsp mustard
- 1/4 tsp smoked paprika

Instructions:

1. **Prepare the beans**: In a medium saucepan, combine the baked beans, BBQ sauce, brown sugar, onion, bacon (if using), mustard, and smoked paprika.
2. **Simmer**: Bring the mixture to a simmer over medium heat. Cook for 15-20 minutes, stirring occasionally, until the flavors meld and the beans are thickened.
3. **Serve**: Serve the BBQ baked beans hot as a side dish at your BBQ.

Grilled Cajun Fish Fillets

Ingredients:

- 4 white fish fillets (such as tilapia, snapper, or cod)
- 2 tbsp olive oil
- 1 tbsp Cajun seasoning
- 1/2 tsp garlic powder
- Salt and pepper, to taste
- Lemon wedges, for serving

Instructions:

1. **Season the fish**: Brush the fish fillets with olive oil. Sprinkle Cajun seasoning, garlic powder, salt, and pepper over both sides of the fillets.
2. **Grill the fish**: Preheat the grill to medium-high heat. Grill the fillets for 3-4 minutes per side, until the fish is opaque and easily flakes with a fork.
3. **Serve**: Serve the grilled Cajun fish with lemon wedges on the side.

Grilled Peach Salad

Ingredients:

- 4 ripe peaches, halved and pitted
- 2 cups mixed greens (arugula, spinach, or baby kale)
- 1/4 cup crumbled goat cheese or feta cheese
- 1/4 cup candied pecans
- 2 tbsp balsamic glaze
- 1 tbsp olive oil
- Salt and pepper, to taste

Instructions:

1. **Grill the peaches**: Preheat the grill to medium heat. Brush the peach halves with a little olive oil and season with salt and pepper. Grill for 3-4 minutes, cut side down, until they have grill marks and are softened.
2. **Assemble the salad**: In a large bowl, combine the mixed greens, grilled peach halves (sliced if desired), crumbled cheese, and candied pecans.
3. **Serve**: Drizzle with balsamic glaze and serve immediately as a light and fresh side dish or main course.

Grilled Lemon Herb Chicken

Ingredients:

- 4 boneless, skinless chicken breasts
- 2 tbsp olive oil
- Juice of 1 lemon
- 2 cloves garlic, minced
- 1 tsp dried oregano
- 1 tsp dried thyme
- Salt and pepper, to taste

Instructions:

1. **Marinate the chicken**: In a bowl, whisk together olive oil, lemon juice, garlic, oregano, thyme, salt, and pepper. Coat the chicken breasts with the marinade and let it sit for 30 minutes to 1 hour.
2. **Grill the chicken**: Preheat the grill to medium-high heat. Grill the chicken for 6-7 minutes per side, or until fully cooked and the internal temperature reaches 165°F (75°C).
3. **Serve**: Serve the grilled lemon herb chicken with your favorite sides.

BBQ Grilled Portobello Burgers

Ingredients:

- 4 large Portobello mushroom caps
- 2 tbsp olive oil
- 1/4 cup BBQ sauce
- 1/4 tsp garlic powder
- Salt and pepper, to taste
- 4 burger buns
- Lettuce, tomato, and pickles for topping (optional)

Instructions:

1. **Prepare the mushrooms**: Preheat the grill to medium-high heat. Remove the stems from the Portobello caps and brush them with olive oil, BBQ sauce, garlic powder, salt, and pepper.
2. **Grill the mushrooms**: Grill the mushrooms, gill side down, for 5-7 minutes. Flip them over and grill for an additional 3-4 minutes until tender.
3. **Assemble the burgers**: Place the grilled mushrooms on burger buns. Top with lettuce, tomato, pickles, or any other toppings you prefer.
4. **Serve**: Serve the BBQ grilled Portobello burgers as a hearty, vegetarian alternative to classic burgers.

www.ingramcontent.com/pod-product-compliance
Lightning Source LLC
LaVergne TN
LVHW081331060526
838201LV00055B/2571